THE APPROACH

AN EVANGELISM

WORKBOOK

YOUR NAME HERE

Welcome to Evangelism 101!

I'm Bishop Jeff, your coach. In this book, you'll find tools to become an effective witness for Christ. Open your mind and let the Holy Spirit guide you with understanding and revelation. Our approach to winning souls is gentle and attentive to everyone's needs. Walk with me, express yourself freely, and jot down useful notes. These tools will add to your mission. Enjoy the journey!

Jeff Briscoe

"Every Christian needs this book to deepen their faith, understand their calling, and spread the Gospel. This devotional provides practical steps, reflective questions, and inspirational teachings to empower you to live boldly for Christ and make a lasting impact in God's kingdom."

FAITH2FAITHBOOKS.COM

TABLE OF CONTENTS

DAY - 01 - GO FORWARD   7

DAY - 02 - BE ATTENTIVE   15

DAY - 03 - EVANGELIZE   23

DAY - 04 - BE READY   31

DAY - 05 - WATCHFUL   39

DAY - 06 - CRY OUT   49

DAY - 07 - AT THE APPOINTED TIME   57

DAY - 08 - JUSTICE   65

DAY - 09 - CALLED TO THE HARVEST   73

DAY - 10 - LABORERS NEEDED   81

DAY - 11 - WALKING IN AUTHORITY   89

DAY - 12 - THE GREAT COMMISSION   97

DAY - 13 - ALWAYS WITH US   105

DAY - 14 - EMPOWERED TO EMPOWER   113

DAY - 15 - REPENT AND BE BAPTIZED   121

The Approach

DAY - 01

GO FORWARD

SCRIPTURE

"And ye shall know that I am in the midst of Israel, and that I am the Lord your God, and none else: and my people shall never be ashamed." - Joel 2:27

"Trust and move forward with God."

ACTION WORD

PARTNERSHIP

What does it mean to you to partnership with the Lord? Think about the significance.

_____

_____

_____

_____

_____

_____

_____

_____

_____

INSTRUCTION

We can't do anything without Jesus. The whole idea of evangelism is God's plan for reconciliation, which is what this ministry is all about. When we think of evangelism, it means to gather. It was God's intent to gather mankind back to Himself after the fall.

Everyone is to evangelize; no believer is exempt. So, as believers, we are to acknowledge that God is with us. Once we acknowledge that He is with us, we realize that we have a partnership to bring souls to Christ. We were called to be witnesses. We are dealing with three things: the voice of God, the voice of the enemy, and our voice. We have to learn to separate and find the voice of reason, which is God's voice. There is a way that seems right unto man but after is destruction (Proverbs 14:12, KJV). We can have a good idea, but that doesn't mean it's a God idea.

ACTION

Trust that God is with you and go forward to do the work of gathering others unto the Lord. Take intentional steps to share the gospel and invite others to experience the love and salvation of Jesus Christ.

MEDITATION

What am I doing to learn to know the voice of God? Is there anything else I need to do to better hear and follow His guidance?

NOTES

NOTES

NOTES

DAY - 02

BE ATTENTIVE

SCRIPTURE

"And it shall come to pass afterward, that I will pour out my spirit upon all flesh; and your sons and your daughters shall prophesy, your old men shall dream dreams, your young men shall see visions:" - Joel 2:28

"Discern God's voice and receive His Spirit."

ACTION WORD

MINISTER

How can you minister to others in your daily life? Reflect on your unique gifts and opportunities.

_____
_____
_____
_____
_____
_____
_____
_____
_____
_____

INSTRUCTION

These verses are our instructions from God. His plan was to pour out His Spirit on all of us. It's important to note that "He," meaning God, will pour it out on sons and daughters. Then He gives a generational breakdown of who He will use to accomplish His will: the older men will dream dreams, and the young men will see visions. Remember that the outpouring isn't just for the pulpit. God will pour out His Spirit on those who will minister, whether they serve in the house of God or in the streets, both men and women. This verse dispels the notion that women can't preach. The outpouring is supernatural, and it's God's intention for the world to witness it.

There is only one Spirit, and God will pour it out upon His people. When we receive the Spirit, we are all connected. Everything isn't on God; we are called to be His hands and feet, so we have the responsibility and accountability to put the things we were called to do into action. If you know God called you to ministry, what are you waiting for? We have to stop waiting; the devil isn't waiting to send people to hell, so why aren't we showing up? We have work to do.

Proverbs 29:18 says, "Where there is no vision, the people perish: but he that keepeth the law, happy is he." One of the first things God gives when He pours out His Spirit is vision because we need to discern what the Spirit of God is saying to His church. If you don't have vision, stir up the gift through reading your Bible, prayer, fasting, and the laying on of hands.

ACTION

Be attentive to the Spirit of God because He plans to pour out His Spirit. Do you have vision? If not, stir it up.

MEDITATION

What am I doing to stir up the gift in me? Have I been consistent? If not, what areas do I need to address?

_____
_____
_____
_____
_____
_____
_____
_____
_____
_____

NOTES

NOTES

DAY - 03

EVANGELIZE

SCRIPTURE

"And also upon the servants and upon the handmaids in those days will I pour out my spirit." - Joel 2:29

ACTION WORD

SERVE

What does serving others mean to you? Think about how you can serve in both small and significant ways.

_____
_____
_____
_____
_____
_____
_____
_____
_____
_____
_____

INSTRUCTION

A handmaid is a personal maid or female servant, and they are vital to society because their purpose is to serve or assist. All the women who feel like they have been disqualified by the church, that's a lie. God has not disqualified you but included you. Those who serve are just as important to God as those who lead. In truth, all of us are called to be servants. We are no longer waiting on the Lord; we have received the instructions.

We must understand the difference between preaching and witnessing. When you receive the Spirit, you automatically become a witness. Many who are called to preach often feel like they have to preach or talk "at" people, but proper protocol involves talking to them. If we prejudge everyone and send them all to hell without due process, what did Jesus die for? We have vision to warn people of the wrath to come, lest their blood be on our hands. We are not here to ensure the downfall of anyone, but to urge men and women to run for their lives. Although there are many people in Hell and on their way It was never God's will that any man should perish; His will is to reconcile man to Himself and deliver as many people from the fire as possible.

There is no torment in love, whatever torments is outside of God. Even those dealing with torments in Hell are outside of God's love. Perfect love casts out fear. We have to learn to give the Word of God without tormenting the ones we give it to. We don't justify sin; people struggle with sin. Some of us know how to sin better than we know how to live holy. So what do you do? You lead by example, and lead with Love. Sometimes it has to be tough, but you always have to be led by the Spirit. We have to teach men and women that God is able to keep that which we commit unto Him against that day. This requires discipline. Holiness is discipline.

ACTION

Go forward. Evangelize. You are an epistle, read by men. Live life the way God intended.

MEDITATION

How am I living my life as a witness for God? Am I actively sharing His love and message with others?

NOTES

NOTES

DAY - 04

BE READY

SCRIPTURE

"And I will shew wonders in the heavens and in the earth, blood, and fire, and pillars of smoke." - Joel 2:30

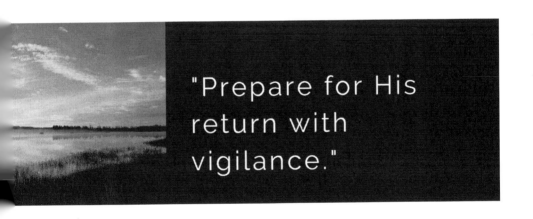

ACTION WORD

ALERT

How can you warn others about the importance of salvation? Think about the balance between urgency and compassion.

_____
_____
_____
_____
_____
_____
_____
_____
_____
_____

INSTRUCTION

We are to warn people of the "evil day" and compel them to come to Christ while they still have time. Ezekiel 3:18 says, "When I say unto the wicked, Thou shalt surely die; and thou givest him not warning, nor speakest to warn the wicked from his wicked way, to save his life; the same wicked man shall die in his iniquity; but his blood will I require at thine hand." Having vision comes with a price, so when the word of God comes to you, you need to warn people of their sins. God always sends warning before judgment, so it's up to us to be ready and watchful.

What if you aren't living the way God calls you to and you see a warning sign? You still have a responsibility, whether you are living right or not, to give the warning. Do you think the people in the city when the enemy comes to destroy it cares if the person who rings the bell is right with God or not? Even ministers don't always have it all together, but they still have to do what God called them to do. Even backsliders need to tell the world of God, not in a way to fit their situations, but in the way that God intended. Yes, even backsliders get blood on their hands. But backslider beware, when you give the warning, it's a two-edged sword; it cuts coming and going. It's best to give it while you are right with God, but if you aren't, still give it and pray that God delivers you.

ACTION

Be ready! Cry loud and spare not.

MEDITATION

Am I watching for the warning signs? Am I warning others only to fall victim of the same destruction I'm broadcasting?

NOTES

NOTES

NOTES

DAY - 05

BE WATCHFUL

SCRIPTURE

"The sun shall be turned into darkness, and the moon into blood, before the great and the terrible day of the Lord come." - Joel 2:31

ACTION WORD

VIGILANCE

What does spiritual vigilance look like for you? Consider areas where you need to be more alert.

INSTRUCTION

The signs of the times are here. Now is the day of salvation; be watchful because God's mercy has an expiration date. We have to warn people while we have time. Think of your family members and even the people you randomly see. Who can abide in the wrath of God? There is a day when the Lord of the harvest shall separate the righteous from the unrighteous. The Son does His job, and then the Father comes to do His final judgment. It is a day to be feared by all, but there is hope for all those who heed the warnings.

We don't want to sit on what God gives us. Tell it all. We wouldn't want anyone to be caught in the wrath of God; we want to make sure we warn as many people as possible. Let's stop sparing the feelings of our loved ones just to stay on good terms with them. Will God be on good terms with you if you neglect to warn?

The prophet Joel's vision of the sun turning into darkness and the moon into blood is a reminder of the impending day of the Lord. It's like a wake-up call, showing us how urgent and serious our times are. We can easily fall into thinking we have plenty of time, but scripture tells us that the day of the Lord will come like a thief in the night (1 Thessalonians 5:2).

These last days, signs are all around us. They aren't just random events; they are divine signals urging us to prepare and stay vigilant. Our watchfulness is not just for our benefit but for the salvation of those around us. As we see these signs, our hearts should be moved with compassion and a sense of urgency to share the gospel.

Again, think about the people in your life—family, friends, coworkers, and even strangers you pass by daily. Each one is a soul that God loves and wants to save. Knowing how severe God's coming judgment is, how can we stay silent? Our silence can have eternal consequences. We must speak the truth in love, even if it means having uncomfortable conversations. The Apostle Paul reminds us in Ephesians 4:15 to speak the truth in love, growing in every way more and more like Christ.

Remember, our warning is an act of love. Imagine a firefighter seeing a house on fire and not warning the occupants because he didn't want to disturb them. How tragic would that be? In the same way, we must be willing to sound the alarm, motivated by love and a deep concern for the eternal destiny of others.

God's mercy is abundant, but it is not limitless. There is a day when His mercy will be replaced by judgment. Today, we have the chance to make a difference. Let us not take this responsibility lightly. Ask God for boldness, wisdom, and a heart filled with His love to reach out to those who are lost.

ACTION

Be watchful until the end.

MEDITATION

Have you been guilty of sparing a person's feelings and not telling them what God is requiring? Would you be alright with knowing that that person died in an unfit condition?

NOTES

NOTES

NOTES

DAY - 06

CRY OUT

SCRIPTURE

"And it shall come to pass, that whosoever shall call on the name of the Lord shall be delivered: for in mount Zion and in Jerusalem shall be deliverance, as the Lord hath said, and in the remnant whom the Lord shall call." - Joel 2:32

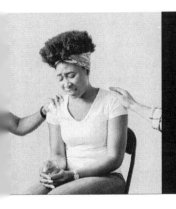

"Surrender and persist in seeking God."

ACTION WORD

SURRENDER

What areas of your life do you need to surrender to God? Reflect on the freedom that comes with surrender.

_____

_____

_____

_____

_____

_____

_____

_____

_____

_____

INSTRUCTION

The only way to escape the judgment to come is to accept Jesus as your Lord and Savior. He isn't just a good teacher or some prophet that lived many years ago. He must be Lord over your life. You have to be obedient to the will of the Spirit. To accept this salvation, you have to be humble. It's a surrender.

Joel's message is clear: deliverance comes to those who call on the name of the Lord. This is not a passive act but an urgent, heartfelt cry for help. Remember the thief on the cross—he didn't have the liberty to whisper what he had to say to Jesus; he cried out. He had nothing to offer, no good deeds to boast about, and no time to make amends. All he had was a cry for mercy, and Jesus responded with grace.

The blind man, Bartimaeus, refused to be silenced—he cried out as well. Although he was told to be silent he shouted even louder, "Son of David, have mercy on me!" (Mark 10:48). His persistence and transparency brought him healing and sight. Those who come to God can't hide their need for salvation; they have to be transparent.

When leading others to Christ, we must remember to do it with love and compassion. The Bible says that Jesus was often moved with compassion when He dealt with the people He ministered to.

He saw the crowds and had compassion on them because they were harassed and helpless, like sheep without a shepherd (Matthew 9:36). Our approach should be the same—full of love, understanding, and urgency.

God's judgment is real, and it's coming. But His deliverance is also real, and it's available to all who call on His name. This is our hope and the hope we must share with others. We can't afford to be silent or complacent. The stakes are too high. There is a reward for obeying the word of God—you get to escape.

ACTION

Cry out to God. Walk in humility. Lead with love.

MEDITATION

Who have you helped to escape the wrath of God? Let's not look at years ago; let's look at this year, this month, even today. The harvest is plenteous but the laborers are few.

NOTES

NOTES

DAY - 07

AT THE APPOINTED TIME

SCRIPTURE

"In those days and at that time, when I restore the fortunes of Judah and Jerusalem." - Joel 3:1

ACTION WORD

ENDURE

How do you handle periods of waiting in your life? Reflect on what God might be teaching you during these times.

INSTRUCTION

In our lives, we often seek an immediate answer or a quick fix to our problems. We live in a world that values instant gratification, where waiting is seen as an inconvenience. However, as believers, we are reminded that God has a perfect timing for everything, including the restoration of our spiritual inheritance. Just as God promised to restore Judah and Jerusalem, He promises to restore us. This restoration is not about worldly wealth or material gain, but about bringing us closer to Him, to our true inheritance in His kingdom.

It's important to understand that our journey through life is a process, one that unfolds according to God's divine timing, not ours. Trusting in this timing means recognizing that every moment of waiting is part of a larger plan designed for our good. It requires us to have faith that God is always at work, even when we cannot see it. He is preparing everything at the appointed time for our spiritual renewal and growth.

During the times of waiting, it is easy to become discouraged or impatient. We might wonder why our prayers are not answered immediately or why we must endure certain trials. But remember, the period of waiting is not a passive time. It is an active period of preparation, faith, and learning to trust in God's plan for your life.

In these moments, God is molding us, shaping our character, and strengthening our faith. He uses these times to teach us patience, reliance on Him, and the importance of aligning our desires with His will.

Waiting on God's timing helps us to develop a deeper relationship with Him. It is during these periods that we often draw closer to God, seeking His presence, guidance, and comfort. We learn to depend on His promises and to find peace in His sovereignty. The process of waiting becomes a transformative journey that brings us into a closer and more intimate relationship with our Creator.

So, as we navigate the ups and downs of life, let's remember that God's timing is perfect. His plans for us are far greater than we can imagine, and His timing is always for our ultimate good. Trust in Him, be patient, and allow the waiting periods to be times of spiritual growth and preparation for the work.

ACTION

Trust in God's perfect timing. When we trust, we are actively surrendering our desires and expectations to God's divine schedule. Use this time of waiting to deepen your relationship with God. Engage in prayer, study His word, and reflect on His past faithfulness. Consider how He has worked in your life before and hold onto those memories as a source of hope and assurance.

MEDITATION

Acknowledge God's presence. Love the Lord with all your heart, and with all thy soul, and with all thy mind and strength (Mark 12:30). This means dedicating your entire being to Him, trusting Him completely, and knowing that His plans for you are good. Reflect on times of waiting.

NOTES

NOTES

DAY - 08

JUSTICE

SCRIPTURE

"I will gather all nations and bring them down to the Valley of Jehoshaphat. There I will put them on trial for what they did to my inheritance, my people Israel, because they scattered my people among the nations and divided up my land." - Joel 3:2

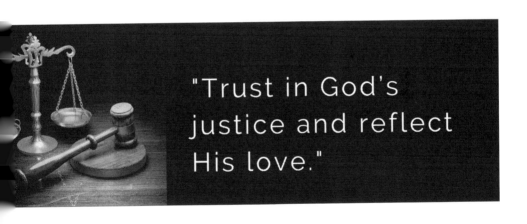

"Trust in God's justice and reflect His love."

ACTION WORD

TRUST

Do you trust in God's perfect justice and timing? Consider how trusting God changes your perspective on suffering and correction.

_____
_____
_____
_____
_____
_____
_____
_____
_____
_____
_____

INSTRUCTION

It's amazing to see that God would use a people to punish His people, and then He would turn around and punish the people He used to inflict the punishment. This shows God's perfect justice. We can't get disheartened when we are chastised because that is a sign of His love. Hebrews 12:11 says, "Now no chastening for the present seemeth to be joyous, but grievous: nevertheless afterward it yieldeth the peaceable fruit of righteousness unto them which are exercised thereby." When God doesn't correct you, you should be worried because, in being corrected, He deals with you as a son.

Have you ever known someone to inflict suffering because they feel it's needed? That's a bad place to be in. You don't want to be the one being judged for the suffering you caused. God says vengeance is His. The Bible says render not evil for evil. My intent to make you suffer is one thing, but God rendering the suffering is another. Offenses will come, but woe unto those through whom they come.

God cleans us up in steps; it's a process. We never want to inflict pain on others during this process. The potter is the one who molds the vessel, not the other pots. If another pot tries to touch a vessel on the wheel, it can be distorted or broken. We, as the people of God, need to let God work on individuals. It's not our job.

ACTION

Watch your posture. Be mindful of your mindset and attitude towards others. Remember, it is God who molds and shapes us. Trust in His process and avoid taking matters into your own hands. Reflect on how you respond to others, especially in times of conflict or correction. Seek to be an instrument of peace and love rather than judgment and punishment.

MEDITATION

When dealing with God there is always a posture we should have. This is your mindset. We should believe, submit and receive. When we have the correct posture we can expect things to happen. Consider your attitude in moments of correction and discipline. Are you open to God's molding, or do you resist? Trust that His corrections are meant to bring about righteousness and peace in your life.

NOTES

NOTES

NOTES

DAY - 09

CALLED TO THE HARVEST

SCRIPTURE

"Then saith he unto his disciples, The harvest truly is plenteous, but the labourers are few;" - Matthew 9:37

ACTION WORD

AVAILABILITY

How can you make yourself more available to God's call? Reflect on areas in your life where you can be more open to serving others.

INSTRUCTION

The harvest is the world, outside of the four walls of the church. When Jesus spoke of this scripture, He was looking at the crowds that would flock to hear Him preach. This symbolizes the many people ready to hear and receive God's Word; that have open minds and hearts. However, there is a shortage of laborers ready to bring in this harvest. This scripture is a call to action for each of us. It's an invitation to step into the fields of our families, communities, and beyond, to share the gospel with a dying world. Being a laborer for God doesn't require special qualifications; it requires a willing heart and a vessel ready to be used by God to touch the lives of others.

Jesus' words remind us that the need is great, and there are opportunities everywhere. People all over are searching for meaning, hope, and truth. They are ready to receive the good news, but there are not enough workers to reach them all. This is where we come in. Each of us has a role to play in God's plan of salvation. Whether it's through sharing our testimony, offering a kind word, or extending a helping hand, we can all contribute to the harvest.

Sometimes we might feel inadequate or unprepared to take on this mission. But remember, God does not call the qualified; He qualifies the called.

All He needs is our willingness to step out in faith and be used by Him. Our availability is more important than our ability. When we make ourselves available to God, He will provide the strength, wisdom, and opportunities we need to make a difference.

ACTION

Make yourself available to God. Reflect on your daily life and consider where you can be a laborer for the harvest. Are there people around you who need to hear about God's love? Are there opportunities to serve and share the gospel? Be open to the leading of the Holy Spirit and ready to step out in faith. Even small acts of kindness and sharing can have a significant impact on someone's life.

MEDITATION

Am I focused and standing on my watch? Reflect on your commitment to God's call. Are you attentive to the needs around you and ready to respond? Ask God to help you be vigilant and proactive in your mission. Trust that He will guide you and provide the opportunities to be a laborer in His harvest.

NOTES

NOTES

DAY - 10

LABORERS NEEDED

SCRIPTURE

"Pray ye therefore the Lord of the harvest, that he will send forth labourers into his harvest." - Matthew 9:38

"Pray for the laborers in God's vineyard."

ACTION WORD

INTERCEDE

How can you intercede for more laborers in God's harvest? Reflect on the importance of prayer in supporting the work of the kingdom.

_____
_____
_____
_____
_____
_____
_____
_____
_____
_____

INSTRUCTION

The instruction from Scripture is clear: we are called to pray for laborers to be sent into the world. This is not just a simple request but a heartfelt intercession for people to be willing and ready to do the work of the Lord. It's about asking God to touch hearts and ignite a passion for serving Him and a desire to see His kingdom come. We must understand that the work of the kingdom is bigger than us and requires many hands. Our prayers should be that more people rise up and join the battle that is going on for the soul.

When we pray for laborers, we are partnering with God in His plan for salvation. We are acknowledging that the need is great and that we cannot do it alone. This is a call to unity among believers, encouraging each other to step forward and fulfill the Great Commission. The Gospel will be spread to all corners of the earth, but it's through us.

Taking action means living out the scripture and aligning our will with God's will. When we obediently follow what the Bible teaches and submit ourselves to God's plan, we pave the way for a fruitful harvest. This involves not just praying but also actively participating in God's work, whether it's through sharing the Gospel, serving others, or using our talents for His glory.

It means being available and ready to go where God sends us, doing what He calls us to do. By stepping out in faith, we become the answers to the prayers for laborers.

ACTION

Make yourself available to God and be ready to serve in whatever capacity He calls you. Reflect on how you can contribute to the harvest in your daily life.

MEDITATION

- Prayer is powerful: Remember to pray fervently for God to raise up laborers for His harvest.
- Obedience leads to blessings: When we obey God's commands and follow His leading, there will be blessings and growth in His kingdom.
- Focus on God's will: Keep your eyes fixed on fulfilling God's will, seeking His guidance and direction in all that you do.

NOTES

NOTES

DAY - 11

WALKING IN AUTHORITY

SCRIPTURE

"And Jesus came and spake unto them, saying, All power is given unto me in heaven and in earth." - Matthew 28:18

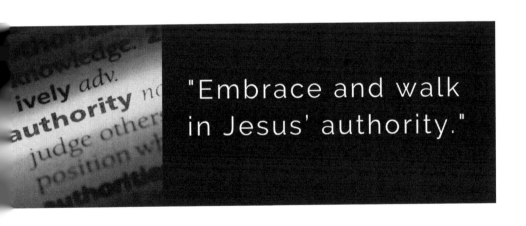

"Embrace and walk in Jesus' authority."

ACTION WORD

REPRESENT

In what ways do you represent Jesus in your daily interactions? Consider how you can better reflect His authority and love.

INSTRUCTION

Jesus was assuring His disciples that He has all authority in heaven and on earth. This is powerful because it means Jesus is in charge of everything, everywhere. Knowing this should change how we live. We need to take Jesus' teachings seriously and live with the confidence that comes from His authority.

Think about it: Jesus has power over every situation we face. His words are our guide, His commands our mission, and His power our strength. When He told His disciples this, He was preparing them to go out and make more disciples (Matthew 28:19-20). This mission is still for us today. We are called to live boldly for Jesus, share His message, and serve others not because we know He is in control, but because we love Him.

Living under Jesus' authority also means we have power in spiritual battles. Ephesians 6:10-11 tells us to be strong in the Lord and in the power of His might, putting on the full armor of God. This means we are not helpless against evil. This same authority gives us victory over sin, temptation, and the enemy.

This authority should also comfort us. When we face hard times or feel afraid, we can remember that Jesus is in charge. His power reaches to the places we can't go so we don't have to worry.

So, as we go through our day, we should remember that we carry an unmatched authority with us. Whether at work, at home, or in our communities, we represent Him. This should give us the courage to take steps of faith, speak truth, and serve others with love.

ACTION

Embrace the authority of Jesus Christ in your daily life. Step out in faith to share the gospel, pray for others, and serve with confidence, knowing that you are backed by the authority of Christ. Reflect on specific areas where you can exercise this authority to impact those around you and bring glory to God.

MEDITATION

Remember the words of Jesus Christ, let them guide your actions and decisions. Reflect on them. Trust Him as you navigate your daily challenges and opportunities, while seeking to gain souls for the Kingdom.

NOTES

NOTES

DAY - 12

THE GREAT COMMISSION

SCRIPTURE

"Go ye therefore, and teach all nations, baptizing them in the name of the Father, and of the Son, and of the Holy Ghost:" - Matthew 28:19

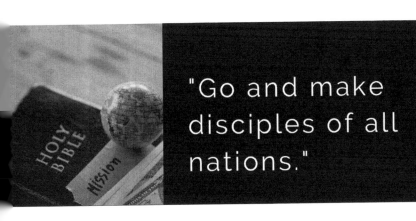

ACTION WORD

GO

How can you actively respond to Jesus' command to "Go"? Reflect on ways you can step out of your comfort zone to share the Gospel.

_____
_____
_____
_____
_____
_____
_____
_____
_____

INSTRUCTION

"Go ye therefore" – Jesus is giving a clear and direct mission to His disciples. He's pointing them towards the purpose of their calling: to spread the Gospel to all nations. The instruction here is action-oriented. It's a call to step out of our comfort zones and engage in the mission Jesus has entrusted to us.

This verse is often referred to as the Great Commission. It's not just a suggestion; it's a command. Jesus is telling us to be proactive in our faith, to go out into the world and make disciples. This involves teaching, baptizing, and guiding people into a relationship with God. It's a mission that requires dedication, courage, and a willingness to serve.

Jesus doesn't just send us out without guidance or support. He promises to be with us always, even to the end of the age (Matthew 28:20). Knowing that we have His presence and power dwelling within us should give us the confidence to carry out this mission. We are not alone in this task; we are empowered by the Holy Spirit to fulfill our calling.

When we think about the word "Go," it signifies movement and initiative. It means we need to be active, not passive, in sharing our faith. Whether it's within our communities, workplaces, or even reaching out to other cultures and nations, we are called to make an impact for the Kingdom of God.

ACTION

Take proactive steps to share the Gospel. Reflect on where you can make a difference – in your family, community, or even globally. Be intentional about teaching others about Jesus, offering to pray for them, and sharing your testimony.

MEDITATION

Throughout your day, think on the words of Jesus. The Bible says, "Trust in the Lord with all thine heart and lean not to your own understanding; in all your ways acknowledge Him, and He shall direct your paths" (Proverbs 3:5-6). When Jesus says, "Go," just do it. Be like Nike – take action without hesitation, trusting that God will guide and support you in every step you take.

_____

_____

_____

_____

_____

_____

_____

_____

_____

NOTES

NOTES

DAY - 13

ALWAYS WITH US

SCRIPTURE

"Teaching them to observe all things whatsoever I have commanded you: and, lo, I am with you always, even unto the end of the world. Amen." - Matthew 28:20

"Live with the assurance of Jesus' presence."

ACTION WORD

TRUST

Do you trust in Jesus' promise to be with you always? Consider how this assurance can give you confidence to carry out your mission.

INSTRUCTION

We have to learn to pay attention to Jesus, listen, and follow His directions. Jesus instructs us not only to go and make disciples but also to teach them to observe everything He has commanded. Our role is to help others grow in their faith by following Jesus' teachings, not just to introduce them to Christ but to guide them in living out His commandments.

This involves modeling a Christ-like life and demonstrating obedience to His teachings. Jesus reassures us with a powerful promise: "I am with you always, even unto the end of the world." This assurance gives us confidence to carry out our mission, knowing that He is always with us, providing strength and guidance.

As we strive to follow Jesus' teachings, we must walk in humility and have a heart willing to serve. Jesus displayed this in washing the feet of His disciples and serving others selflessly. When we humble ourselves and serve others, we reflect the love and grace of Christ. This not only strengthens us but also inspires those around us to seek a deeper relationship with Him.

In addition, we must remain steadfast in prayer and study of the Scriptures. These practices keep us grounded in our faith and open to the Holy Spirit's guidance. When we immerse ourselves in God's Word and maintain a constant dialogue with Him through prayer, we equip ourselves to face challenges and remain faithful in our mission. Remember, the journey of faith is continuous, and through persistent prayer and study, we draw closer to Jesus and become more effective in making disciples for His kingdom.

ACTION

Move forward confidently, trusting that God is with you in every step. Whether you feel His presence or not, have faith in His promise. Actively teach and live out His commandments, showing others how to do the same.

MEDITATION

Remember and refer to the word of God to build your confidence in doing His will. Meditate on His promises as your source of strength and encouragement.

NOTES

NOTES

DAY - 14

EMPOWERED TO EMPOWER

SCRIPTURE

"And Jesus said unto them, Come ye after me, and I will make you to become fishers of men."
- Mark 1:17

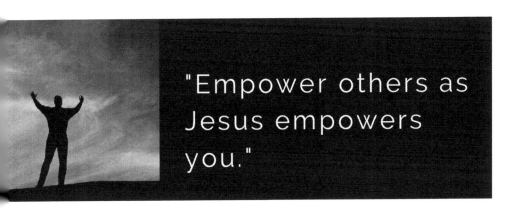

ACTION WORD

BOLDNESS

Do you pray for boldness to share your faith? Think about how you can rely on the Holy Spirit to guide your words and actions.

_____
_____
_____
_____
_____
_____
_____
_____
_____
_____

INSTRUCTION

Imagine standing by the sea, hearing the waves gently crash against the shore. Jesus approaches you with a simple yet powerful invitation: "Come after me." In that moment, everything changes. You are no longer just a bystander; you are called to a greater purpose. Jesus promises to transform you into a fisher of men, someone who will bring others to Him.

This calling is not just for the disciples but for all of us. As believers, we are empowered by Jesus to empower others. He gives us the strength, the words, and the courage to share His love with the world. Our mission is to spread the Good News, to reach out to those who are lost, and to lead them to the light of Christ.

Take a moment to think about when you first felt called to follow Jesus. How has He transformed your life since then? Write down your thoughts in a journal. Ask God to give you the boldness to share your faith with others. Pray for opportunities to speak about Jesus and for the Holy Spirit to guide your words and actions.

I'm not telling you to go rent out a stadium and call the city, Identify one person in your life who needs to hear the Good News. Reach out to them this week. It could be a friend, a coworker, or even a stranger. Share your testimony and the love of Christ with them. After you've done that, find another, and then another until evangelism becomes a part of who you are at your core. Don't stop reaching out, keep.

ACTION

Trust that God is with you and go forward to gather others unto the Lord. Share the gospel intentionally and invite others to experience Jesus' love and salvation. Reflect on how Jesus empowers you to empower others.

MEDITATION

Am I actively sharing my faith? How can I be more confident in evangelizing? Who needs to hear the Good News from me this week?

NOTES

NOTES

DAY - 15

REPENT AND BE BAPTIZED

SCRIPTURE

"Then Peter said unto them, Repent, and be baptized every one of you in the name of Jesus Christ for the remission of sins, and ye shall receive the gift of the Holy Ghost." - Acts 2:38

"Repent, be baptized, and receive the Holy Ghost."

ACTION WORD

GUIDE

In what ways can you guide others through the process of repentance and baptism? Think about how you can support and mentor them on their spiritual journey.

INSTRUCTION

In this scripture, we find the core of the apostles' doctrine and the result of everything Jesus taught them. From The Great Commission in Matthew 28 to this statement in Acts 2:38, Peter is revealing the plan that God has for all mankind. Salvation comes by Jesus, and it is up to each individual to take action and accountability.

Peter instructs us to repent and be baptized in the name of Jesus Christ for the remission of sins. This is not just a symbolic act; it is a powerful step of faith and obedience. Baptism represents the outward physical part of receiving salvation. When we are baptized, we become one with the Father through the Son, symbolizing our death to sin and resurrection to a new life in Christ. As the Bible says, without the shedding of blood, there is no remission of sins (Hebrews 9:22).

Through baptism, we receive the forgiveness of our sins, and we are promised the gift of the Holy Ghost. This gift empowers us to live a life pleasing to God and to continue His work on earth. It is essential to understand that baptism is not just a ritual but an act of faith and obedience that connects us deeply with Jesus' sacrifice and resurrection.

As ministers of the Gospel, we have a critical role in leading others to this understanding. We must share the importance of seeking God's forgiveness and committing one's life to Him. Our mission includes guiding others through the process of repentance and baptism, explaining its significance, and encouraging them to take this vital step in their spiritual journey. We also encourage them to receive the Holy Ghost, which empowers them to live a life dedicated to God.

ACTION

Encourage others to repent and be baptized in the name of Jesus Christ. Lead by example, and guide them through understanding and taking these steps.

MEDITATION

Repentance is a daily obligation. Think about how you can effectively communicate these teachings to those you are evangelizing. While evangelizing, don't neglect your need for salvation, one who teaches repentance should do it by example.

NOTES

NOTES

NOTES

NOTES

NOTES

NOTES

NOTES

NOTES

Made in the USA
Middletown, DE
02 October 2024